D1070501

Ayudantes de la comunidad / Helping the Community

¿Qué hacen LOS CARTEROS?
What Do MAIL CARRIERS Do?

Nick Christopher
Traducido por Eida de la Vega

PowerKiDS press

New York

Published in 2016 by The Rosen Publishing Group, Inc.
29 East 21st Street, New York, NY 10010

First Edition

Editor: Katie Kawa
Book Design: Katelyn Heinle
Spanish Translator: Eida de la Vega

Photo Credits: Cover (mail carrier), p. 1 Tetra Images/Getty Images; cover (hands) bymandesigns/Shutterstock.com; back cover Zffoto/Shutterstock.com; p. 5 © iStockphoto.com/BassittART; p. 6 RICHARD HUTCHINGS/ Science Source/Getty Images; pp. 9, 24 (uniform) Kyle Monk/Blend Images/Getty Images; p. 10 (top) © iStockphoto.com/carterdayne; p. 10 (bottom) Migdale Lawrence/Science Source/Getty Images; p. 13 Tupungato/Shutterstock.com; pp. 14, 24 (post office) http://upload.wikimedia.org/wikipedia/commons/d/ d8/LongPointStationHouston.JPG; p. 17 Monkey Business Images/Shutterstock.com; p. 18 mjay/Shutterstock.com; p. 21 William Thomas Cain/Getty Images News/Getty Images; p. 22 © iStockphoto.com/Juanmonino.

Library of Congress Cataloging-in-Publication Data

Christopher, Nick.
 What do mail carriers do? = ¿Qué hacen los carteros? / Nick Christopher.
    pages cm. — (Helping the community = Ayudantes de la comunidad)
Parallel title: Ayudantes de la comunidad.
In English and Spanish.
Includes bibliographical references and index.
ISBN 978-1-4994-0633-7 (library binding)
1. Letter carriers—Juvenile literature. I. Title.
HE6241.C47 2016
383'.1023—dc23

Manufactured in the United States of America

CPSIA Compliance Information: Batch #WS15PK: For Further Information contact Rosen Publishing, New York, New York at 1-800-237-9932

CONTENIDO

CONTENTS

Los carteros nos traen el correo.

Mail carriers bring us mail.

Los carteros también se llevan el correo que queremos enviar a otras personas.

Mail carriers also take the mail we want to send to other people.

Los carteros usan una ropa especial. Se llama **uniforme**.

Mail carriers wear special clothes. This is called a **uniform**.

Los carteros trabajan en ciudades grandes. También trabajan en pueblos pequeños.

Mail carriers work in big cities. They work in small towns, too.

Algunos carteros manejan un camión de correo. Es rojo, blanco y azul.

Some mail carriers drive a mail truck. It is red, white, and blue.

14

La gente puede llevar cartas a la **oficina de correos**. Entonces, los carteros reparten esas cartas.

People can bring letters to a **post office**. Then, mail carriers deliver those letters.

Los carteros usan una bolsa
grande para llevar el correo.

Mail carriers use a big bag
to carry mail.

Los carteros ponen las cartas en los buzones de la gente.

Mail carriers put letters in people's mailboxes.

Los carteros también llevan paquetes. ¡A veces, dentro de los paquetes hay regalos!

Mail carriers bring boxes, too. Sometimes the boxes have gifts inside!

¿Te gusta recibir correo?

Do you like to get mail?

PALABRAS QUE DEBES APRENDER
WORDS TO KNOW

(la) oficina de correos
post office

(el) uniforme
uniform

ÍNDICE / INDEX

SITIOS DE INTERNET / WEBSITES

Due to the changing nature of Internet links, PowerKids Press has developed an online list of websites related to the subject of this book. This site is updated regularly. Please use this link to access the list: www.powerkidslinks.com/htc/mail